SINGING MY MOTHER'S SONG

Rebecca Tantony

R Tantony

Burning Eye

Burning Eye Books
Never Knowingly
Mainstream

Supported using public funding by
**ARTS COUNCIL
ENGLAND**

LOTTERY FUNDED

This edition published by Burning Eye Books 2019

www.burningeye.co.uk
@burningeyebooks

Burning Eye Books
15 West Hill, Portishead, BS20 6LG

ISBN 978 1 911570 62 2

Cover design & illustrations by Anna Higgie

SINGING MY MOTHER'S SONG

Contents

Introduction

Sometimes you don't realise how much you need something until it happens. Until it has moved you into newness, until it has become clear that without it, you were only a part of yourself, a near person, something not quite ready.

My family aren't talkers— some of us don't make sense of the world through words— but we feel it in our bodies regardless. As a child I hungered to understand who they were through language. The older I got, the more questions I asked: of their stories, of their pasts, of their futures.

Whilst some of my mother's siblings still have memories linked to South Africa, where it's said their grandfather once lived, my mother has none. From the age of seven until fourteen, she, along with her siblings, lived in a variety of orphanages in the East End of London. A relationship with her father was maintained for a while, but she never saw her mother again. Handed-down histories of South Africa ended with the loss of family connection.

I believe, through blood and bone, nurture and habit, we carry in our bodies those who came before us. Sometimes we are conscious of this, we see patterns or behaviours replicated, the same mistakes made, the same choices determined by what has come to pass. Other times it isn't as transparent, but we feel drawn somehow. It's as if we are anchored by a perspective that doesn't belong to us; or, at least, one we no longer need to claim as our own personal truth.

Living in a time where the past can be considered and explored, I have become a teenager again, the same one who would watch Twin Peaks in her pyjamas, a notebook in hand, trying to piece together clues and evidence. I have hired genealogists, conducted interviews, married memory and dreams to fill in the gaps. I started the journey in Bristol. It took me to London, then over to South Africa – Cape Town, Port Elizabeth, Queenstown, Johannesburg – and then finally back to Bristol. This collection is to be read as a linear narrative which moves between all of these locations.

I am different as a result of this journey. At times I have felt the dead in my room shake me from sleep. I have been afraid of resurfacing heartache in those I love. I have entered places geographically and metaphorically, that have left me lost and stumbling. We know how to navigate ourselves through the familiar, even when it no longer serves us. When you begin to redefine the world around you it becomes mysterious and unspecified.

Women pass on pieces of who they are, through daughter to mother over and over again. Triumph as much as failure, pain as much as joy, until we stop and examine what is being handed over. Until we look at what needs to be held and what needs to be released. I'm of a generation that has the luxury to be able to do this. I have turned backward and forward, gently picked apart and put together - not because pain needs to be relived, but because it needs to be redefined, with perspective.

Maternal lineage is fascinating and women are powerful. We dream, we heal, we create. We carry the women of before in our actions, in our hearts and on our tongues. In some moments I am further away from understanding who I am, who my mother is. In others we are the same person and I have never felt her closer.

As a result of this exploration, lost family have been reunited, conversations have emerged, memories and stories celebrated. I have gathered the narratives of mothers in all their magnitude from individuals across the globe. I have been contacted by strangers wanting to share their own ancestral journeys. It has become something so much bigger than me and my family story. Sometimes, I think this book has been formed by an imagined daughter, clearing the way ahead before her own birth. Or by whole generations, wanting to look both behind and in front, to finally learn the song of ourselves.

Singing My Mother's Song is for the high and low notes. It's for the wind, carrying the old songs somewhere they can finally rest. It's for the sounds we are brave enough to let leave the body. It's for the new songs, those of change and those of now.

*

Between a Cough and a Cry

1.

this is how it begins / somewhere in my body / there is a caught
song / at times I have felt it sticky on the roof of my mouth
/ tracing itself across my palms / folding my heart into a mess
/ i do not know how to sing it

2.

i was born in the hospital corridor / my mother warned
the nurses she was ready / said i was knocking
down the door / a delivery from the inside / out / they said
she was wrong / that the doctors would know best
when the time came / that a woman who carried two
hearts / could never understand / how life sounds
/ when it calls / itself / home

3.

you were born in london's east end mother / between a cough
and a cry / into the arms of two people / one brown / one white
/ neither of them grasping space / neither of them sure how
to hold on

/ back then you used to sing / aged four your grandfather
would pick at south africa on his guitar and you would send
your lips all over the room / aged six your sister and you learnt
a tune together / voices high and clear / the agony of it keeping
everyone in place for a while

aged seven / when your father left home / that note that kept
diminishing

/ your mother / tried for a year / scrubbing songs from the sink
/ before they took you to aldersbrook orphanage / family shifting
through your skeleton / you stroked your own elbow then / sucked
your own thumb

the silence rushed and the melodies slipped behind the sofa
/ even though you reached a hand back into the dark / there was no
one to be found

4.

there is a caught song somewhere in our bodies mother / i feel
it too / though now it has moved down to my feet / taken me along
the edge of table mountain / onto the brink of port elizabeth's dock

/ it will return itself again / travel the route of our oesophagus
/ one day / we will name its journey / i'm sure we will hear
it calling this time / know when it's ready to stay caught

/

then ready to move us both on

The Songs of Three Women

The woman in white stands atop
the cliffs of Cape Town, and through
a megaphone sets free

two hundred and fifty songs a day
to passing sailors. Some are caught
in teeth, in nets, on the waist of a hull,

others are lost beneath sea and sky.
Her spirit can still be heard if you
scoop an ear to a shell and speak ocean.

*

A woman in solitary confinement,
in a Port Elizabeth cell, waits on a single
mattress in a windowless room.

Dinner gets kicked in through the door
and spilt. When she tries to rescue
the remains, the guard breaks her knuckles.

Her spirit, like a moth to filament,
flickers around a single bulb. The hum
of a new protest song burns her gut.

*

In the orphanage my mother
is called a fussy eater.
When she can't finish her dinner

they serve it cold to her the next day.
Seven years is a long
time of eating yesterdays.

Yesterdays are sour, curdled
and no longer nourish the bones.
Her spirit is hungry –

it has eaten her voice instead.

The Ventriloquist's Voice

---

*In ancient Greece, ventriloquism was a religious practice. The name
comes from Latin and translates roughly as 'to speak from the stomach'.
The ventriloquist would interpret the sounds produced by the stomach,
which were thought to be the voices of the dead.*[1]

The Genealogist has found my great-grandfather in the *Stage*
newspaper. When she tells me I laugh, sure she has written
the wrong man into our history. I report back to my mother
and she fills the phone call with fragmented time. Says,
'It's him. I remember the dummies hung up in their house,
staring at us across the room, their shocked expressions,
their bodies the same size as our own.' In photographs,
my great-grandfather is dressed in burgundy, a brown
bowler hat and thick round glasses. Now he climbs onto
my knee, my tentative hand pressed to his spine, his jaw
slack and open, his story made from other people's silences.
Sooner or later I will know exactly what he yearns to say.
But for now, he is dumbstruck: the man who once threw
his voice away, so someone, someday, would finally call it back.

---

1 Cristiana Giordano. *Migrants in Translation*. Oakland, CA: University of California
Press, 2014

A Flood of Men and a Few Different Languages

I am looking for clues

to find   where in South Africa   my great-grandfather

may have lived

My aunty says she remembers

he spoke a few different languages

In South Africa they speak

isiZulu isiXhosa isiNdebele Sesotho

Sesotho sa Leboa siSwati Xitsonga SASL

Setswana Tshivenda English and Afrikaans

Before the trip I practise saying

Please Great-Grandfather

where are you hiding

in each one

*

My uncle says he remembers a flood of men

arriving into his   grandfather's home

Black white and brown South African men in loud suits

                              they'd smoke and spit in turn

Perhaps they were family   *I was too young to know*

                    but they kept saying

I would be okay

                              if I moved there to South Africa

                I would live as a Cape Coloured boy

not black enough to be a problem   *not white enough to be free*

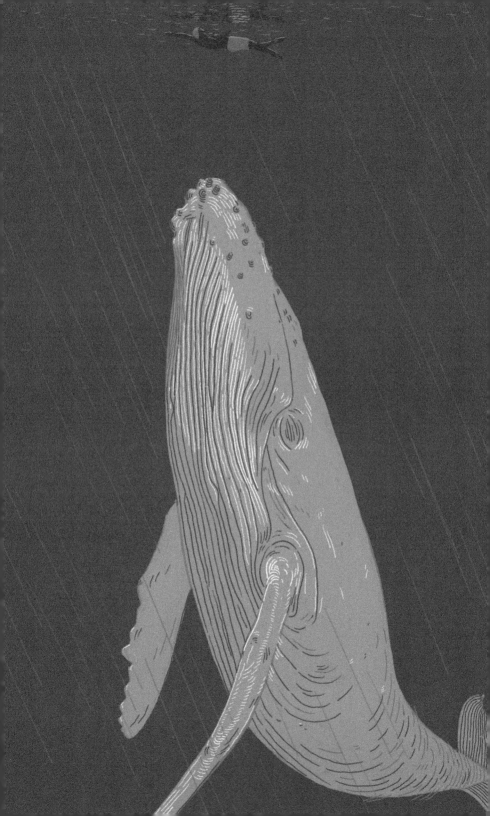

His Strange Kind of Alchemy

In the taxi from the beach back into Cape Town, the driver says Table Mountain is watched over by a huge god. His name is Umlindi Wemingizimu and he was spat out from Thixo, the rib side of the sun. Elements have turned his skin from stone to gold and no matter where you stand he is only ever a shadow behind, casting a watchful light over it all.

The driver's name is Kufar. He is all whispers at first; beyond the music and air rushing through my open window, his words keep passing by, yet the more our journey bends the more his voice heightens.

I don't know how we stumble onto fear; perhaps it's the speed in which the beach vanishes from behind us, the twist of the roads or the forests which we shoot past. Kufar keeps telling me to pray, or repent:

'These bends could be the death of us all. Tell me, have you made mistakes? You can't hide from yourself here,' he says.

He is a self-analyst, documenting his weaknesses, then finding ways to confront and move through them. Not used to the depths of the sea, heart full as a freshly poured drink, he edged towards the water and ran in. 'I made myself swim deeper. I flipped onto my back and looked up at the universe, floated out where the whales and sharks passed through. Every time I go back to that beach I take myself further.'

Kufar moved to Cape Town from Zimbabwe when he was eighteen and now he never wants to return. When he is back home, it all seems too ancient for him, too traditional and old to stay for long.

'I was scared of the townships. We would hear stories in Zimbabwe of gun crime in South Africa. I was frightened to drive past them, so one evening I made myself go. Inside, amongst the tangle of homes, I found friends. Now I visit once a week for braai. We drink beer together, eat chicken and dance to music that squawks through old speakers and slaps us. There is nothing to fear, really, when you step inside and examine it.'

I think of my own examination, the dissection of who I am, who I could be. How my great-grandfather may have left this behind to find something in a country on the other side of Earth.

There were also the spiders, the dark, the loneliness since Kufar now understood how close he could feel to another body. The empty moments that couldn't be filled with conversation and music, the government, the police, the him who remained when distractions had divorced themselves from the hot Cape Town evenings. The him who got angry at injustice, who had been left aged seven to pocket his mother's final words. The him who felt self-conscious while dancing, who didn't make enough money to pay his brother back.

'I have friends from all over the world. Even from Japan. When we were out in a club I spotted pickpockets and I told them – my friends – let me look after your money. I had eight wallets bulging out my jeans. I'm not scared to fight for those I care about.' We are slowing down now, nearly at our temporary home.

How frightening and freeing it is to lose and learn yourself out there, in the people, places, moments of this world. Challenging the conditions that try to keep us tiny, turning both in and out, to see what we are made of.

'Then there is you,' he says. 'Now, that is the biggest fear to conquer. Sometimes I speak to myself, when no one is around. I say you are so unknown, such a strange animal, fuck, you are petrifying.'

I think Kufar then tells me that little by little you discover the multitudes within and see that beyond the anxiety, past the grinding teeth and locked jaw, past the rapid heart and clenched shoulders, beyond it all, is a you so vast and endless it's enough to make you see a god staring back. But I can't be sure. I am too distracted by the outside, followed home by the sun, the moon and that huge mountain, simply unaware of its own magnitude.

Lelethu

In New Brighton Township
Lelethu and I eat meat cooked
on an open fire, potatoes diced
and dressed, the fleshy intestines
of butternut squash. In between

mouthfuls we offer poetry, take turns
to stand and stare at one other's
appetite for words. Every time we pepper
the air, the garden of that bar is paused,
even the chewed food freezes,

and the huddling men digest
our longing. When we finish there
is a gurgle of applause –
ours a shared hunger, to see the world
through our mouths.

This is our first and only
meeting and I spill my reasons
for travelling here: to understand
this part of my heritage, to fill in
the missing bits, and Lelethu says

if South Africa is in your blood,
eventually you will hear it call.
That evening: a banquet before us,
we sit, cut our poems into chunks,
taste every flavour of every mouthful.

Lelethu went completely blind in 2013.
She tells me this right after
she searches my face for language.
'It's a job, isn't it?' she says.
'In both our countries,

through both our songs,
to give a tongue to those
who don't have the chance
to use their own.'
She speaks of her journey.

How much she has been given
since her sight was removed.
When we swap poetry
I hear in our longings,
questions, failures,

triumphs, answers, arrivals,
the raw wonder
of all the women we have
come to be.
And I almost forget

her world is a kaleidoscope
of light and dark, when Lelethu
turns to me and asks,
'You. Now tell me.
What colour are you?'

How Can Everyone Belong to Us?

He says: 'I moved here from Nigeria and became a taxi driver. Because of this car, I hear so many stories. Back home you ask for family history and my cousin will tell the tale of everyone in the village. They are passed from heart to tongue, something offered then shared barefoot on the grass, below the undressing night. Do they change when they are given over, take on different shapes depending on how we bring them back? Who knows? Who cares? All I need is something to help me make sense of who I am now.'

Outside the sky has performed all kinds of moods; it settles on baby blue with a promise of change. The sun has scribbled messages across my cheek. My hands tap my thighs, unlearning a problem I have carried here.

'Make-believe and imagination work for me. You ask for a family story and my cousin will give you a woman who flew, a child who knew how to breathe underwater, and you find your nephew, your sister in them. We call everyone family. That sounds strange to you, doesn't it? Neighbours, friends, even the bank manager no one likes have become heroes.'

Both our bodies are too huge for this car. Our hair too busy with fire. Our tomorrows too unknown to keep them to ourselves, so we gather friends and strangers so to see ourselves through.

'How can everyone belong to us? Is it comforting at all? Why travel so far to collect one thing? There are bits everywhere to hold on to. When you shut your eyes, how does your great-grandfather move when he dances? Do you feel his guidance come through when the slack body has softened, the shell of you cracked, and flooding in are all the women and men of before? Do you call their names, not with syllables and sound, but through the language of remembrance for something familiar?'

I wrote this moment on water so long ago. At least I think I did. Because I have lived it before somewhere, then abandoned it for logic and reason. There is movement in my stomach, something between retching and butterflies. Something of guts.

'I will take you to the National Archive, to where some of us were put on paper, to where your great-grandfather may be named. But, before you walk in, turn your face to the sky. Read it there first, then listen to how it sounds in the market, in the retching dog, taste it in the curve of a papaya. Hear it again in the river, feel it in both the drowning and the rescue. Remember what the water brought. Open them now, your eyes, place them here, in the mirror. Look deeper, right at me. Now, do you see? I have placed his face on my own.'

Lyn

---

said   her mother   was a pain   in the side

she couldn't   quite   shift

so she   replaced her   with angry men

who seemed   to only want   her late

with the   lights out   until she forgot

how the pain   is a hard thing   in the body

that can sometimes   be removed

We are driving   Port Elizabeth   between the bay

and   the bridge   when she says

her mother's song   was her father's sadness

the man   who slept   without   stirring

Her song   the day   she learnt when it was time to leave

how to walk   the thunder   out the front door

yet shut it softly   behind

so to teach   the hate   a lesson

And when that   pain still   followed

the one   which has kept her   strange

to herself   Lyn would come   to this bay

reach a hand   inside

pull then put   an ear   to the heart

of its story   listen   to what it had to say

Once heard   let it   loose

on the sunny side   of a Port Elizabeth afternoon

At the ebb of the shore   she would stare   mesmerised

at that   thin blue line   between

ocean   and sky

Imagine herself   walking   across it   like a tightrope

not really steady   but not quite falling either

In Worship

Today my friends will marry: an English woman, a Xhosa man. I have come to Queenstown for the naming ceremony. I have come to Queenstown to understand ritual. I have come to Queenstown to see love move. His mother is a flurry of swept floors and baked goods. She asks me if I know what it's like to be so excited it hurts. This is the only one of her children's weddings she's been able to attend. During the other two she worked as a maid in Johannesburg for the white families and her son would come with her, sit and watch her clean in the same frenzy she does now. Her son, the TV personality. When we strut into supermarkets the checkout girls choke his name to each other, blush and fan the air in rapture. His mother wants us to pray for their marriage. She brings a Bible over to the table where his new wife and I sit. She has covered the outside of the Bible in a magazine that reads *Johannesburg's Sexiest Stars*. Topless photographs of celebrities dress the spine, swell out onto the front. Her daughter-in-law and I catch each other's eyes, blink laughter back into our bodies, but when we see one of the celebrities is her son, we spill, all liquid and air, barely able to contain ourselves. 'Mama,' his wife and I dribble, 'this is your boy on here, his chest, his flexed arms, his pout,' and she smiles back, half aware of the boldness, half carefree. She asks again: 'Do you know what it is like to be so excited it hurts? After everything we have been through. What it is to see your son wear his skin for an entire country to praise, to look upon in worship?' And yeah, she is right. It does hurt and it hurts and hurts and, in a way, it hasn't stopped hurting since.

Those Rock-Pool Eyes

I can tell the taxi driver has been crying. It's not just his ocean face, those rock-pool eyes, it's the feeling when I enter the car. It's fresh inside, washed clean somehow, like a heavy rain cloud just understood it can finally let go. And it smells like you are in a sweet shop. When I buckle up, ask him what the smell is, his face breaks into sunlight.

'Look behind your head,' he offers. And I cram my eyes over my shoulder to find an entire pineapple, cut at the neck and along the body, all fat and agreeable. 'The best air freshener going,' he says. 'I use them all over my house.'

He is sat in the bathroom. Head flooding into his palms, that same brooding storm hangs ready, it has followed him from room to room. He has hundreds of them here; hung up by the mirror, they remind him of something kinder. There are two by the front door, five lined up in bed, and although they hurt when he forgets and rolls a little too close to the emptiness on her side, the sudden shock is welcomed somehow.

He learnt, like they all did, that big boys don't cry, so at first he made it happen. Poked himself in the ribs, felt the tiniest bit of water gather in each tear duct. Next he watched a romantic film, little streams came then, he would wipe them away with an acute self-awareness. He cried in front of the woman he loved once. Wild and uninhibited, after she had asked him to be a little more expressive. All the practice before was for that one moment, but when he recalled the memory he realised that's when she stopped looking at him fully. That she left him not long after that.

We glide slick and quiet through the back streets of Johannesburg, his car as well kept as a promise. 'There's more.' He winks into the mirror. I find one poking out from under his seat, another below the glovebox. And when the destination arrives, he pulls in, turns around and nods towards the back of my head. 'Don't tell anyone my secret,' he adds.

I wonder if the men in my family have cried. Did they let themselves touch the sweet centre of their own sadness? Did they bottle themselves up or long to be opened? Outside the car, a vendor is calling the city out of his voice. He flips between isiZulu and English. 'Three for two,' he says, holding out a basket full of fruit. 'Mango, nectarine, pineapple?'

As I search for the change in my pocket, the basket tilts and the fruit begins to fall. I reach my hands towards the tumble, catch a pineapple and pull it toward my chest. The vendor and I share a moment, a recognition, a knowing, and I swear he has been carrying that basket for the longest time. Just needing to let it all go. Wearing that ocean face, those rock-pool eyes.

Bones

1.

My mother is the first
and last person I collapse into.

Just before the trip we meet for dinner,
eat balsamic chicken, while I pick her brains

and bones, my hunger for family stories
insatiable. I hear her speak my great-

grandfather the loudest. How he spat phlegm
from an armchair made by his own hands.

The future is a fat space I fill with this unknown
man, behind him a boy, behind the boy a sun,

and I fly away so to face the beginning of time:
Port Elizabeth, Cape Town, the many homes of him.

2.

At the National Archives, I wait in line, say,
'I bet you know every record off by heart,'

And the man behind the counter replies,
'Every record is a heart.'

3.

The Cape of Good Hope feels like falling
and my great-grandfather is a name

that never landed on the page. 'No record
of him here,' the man behind the counter says,

so instead I draw a blank box. I fill
the box with songs taught to me by the land.

I stuff it with watermelons,
migrating whales, fermenting breads,

chakalaka and rooibos tea, with men
who sit on the bench at the bay,

winking at themselves. There he is, look,
dressed up for celebration, tall, grown,

in the heat of a people, his red shoes on,
his smile all tight and slick.

4.

After a month I return to England,
somehow carrying him by hand.

How could a country that moves
this much have held us both in place?

Like I said, as soon as I return, my mother
is the first person I collapse into.

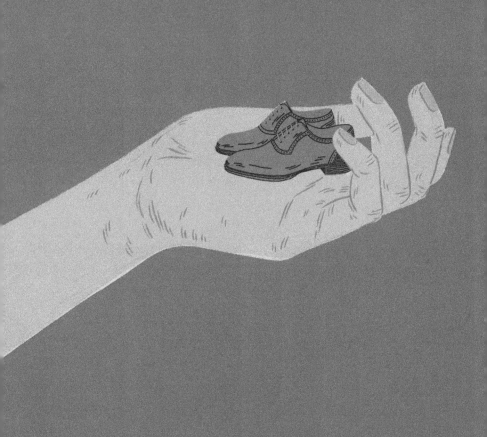

*

These Are the Things I Have Learnt People Leave Behind

Rings too small for chubby fingers
A photograph in which a stranger leans on a bar the same way you
leaned into that boy
Recipes for banana bread
Golden Virginia clinging on to certain jumpers
Certain jumpers
The strange appearance of time
A flowery orange dress that is somehow still in fashion
Feelings you have, though you can't explain them. Like an irrational
fear of whales
A rocking chair now by a window
The wonder of belonging
An ache to be in water
An attic with a trunk of things that you are too afraid to open
A jewellery box with a pirouetting ballerina inside
A great-grandfather clock, donated to the local council by my own
great-grandfather. Now stood outside the entrance to a job centre in
a shopping arcade in Edmonton Green, East London

*

Time is a strange feeling

the Genealogist says, then adds that
before retiring, my great-grandfather
owned three clock shops in London.
He was a specialist, a member
of the Horological Institute, a kind
of inventor. She says he was a sundial.
I imagine him moving in circles.

He was an hourglass,
stood in front of numerals, his hands
pulling the minutes in all directions.
She says he was a clockmaker, winding
the days back. Just like I am doing now.
He was an alarm bell. Then a stopwatch,
pausing time, before starting it again.

Driving Back on Ourselves

In that awkward place where nothing quite fits, we found one another. Knocked shoulders and laughed on meeting. I was trying to call a taxi but the number was engaged and my phone kept losing the fight to keep itself useful.

Of course, some would argue nothing was ever not planned, that the world had pulled us into that same moment for a reason, but those people were often searching for meaning and I was far too practical for that. I had tied my own shoelaces this morning, after all, had paid the electrical bill.

Even though we lived eighteen miles apart, it had been two months since we'd last seen one another. I had wanted to, but was busy, or lazy, or growing into an adult, and so many other things seemed to take the place of our shared time together.

On collision we broke into laughter, then embraced, the smell of her all breakfast tea and hemp hand cream, so very, very familiar.

'Why didn't you ring me for a lift? I told you, call me whenever you need to.'

'I know,' I said, face baby-soft. 'I'm just trying to be responsible, trying to find my own way back.'

I threaded my arm into hers, said, 'But I would love a lift, Mum.'

When we walked towards the car and climbed inside, I slipped my trainers off, clipped on my seatbelt and pulled my knees towards my chest.

'Your legs are too long for the car. You're getting taller all the time.'

'Or you're shrinking?' I laughed, a little girl caught somewhere in my voice. Mum steered her eyes down to her body and back up again.

'So I am,' she said, pulling out of the car park, past the garage and on to the A370.

We drove through all the back-of-the-hand roads, quiet and intimate, fidgeting in our own skin.

'Why don't you sing me a song?' Mum asked. 'Something new.'

'*Twinkle Twinkle*?' I said, and Mum smiled back, the cosmos spilling out of the exhaust. An undertone soon began to fill the car with noise, as we belted our own melody, voices crashing into space.

'Look, cows,' Mum exclaimed once we had finished singing, tapping excitedly at the glass, 'and there's a dog in a winter jacket. Sheep painted blue. Why do they put colours on them?'

I shrugged back in response, asked, 'Are we nearly there yet?' And Mum echoed the sentence, until we threw it between us like a game of air hockey, breaking into pieces, snorting in turn.

Soon Mum was pulling into the drive of a big house. Once parked, the ignition was turned off and Mum moved around so to open the doors, but couldn't, so sat hot and flitting, seemingly stuck. I soon began to cry and, in seeing me so upset, Mum couldn't hold back either, and once started we were both wailing, flooding the car with the saddest parts of ourselves.

Not long after the door clicked open, high-speed hands reached in and pulled us up and out of our own misery.

'Girls, there you are. I thought you were in the garden. Were you playing cars again?' We nodded, throwing shy glances at one another. 'Very sweet, but I told you before, keep at the back of the house, please.'

This time we promised and she walked us round, past the rose bushes, through the bursting honeysuckle. It was next to the rosemary plants that we let go of her hands, skipped across the lawn before finding ourselves cross-legged on the warm ground, waving her goodbye.

'Shall we play a game?' Mum asked.

'Yeah, let's play a game,' I said back.

'Truth or dare. You have to tell me a secret or do something brave.'

'Let's tell secrets,' I said. 'I've been holding onto one for the longest time.' We moved closer to each other's faces, our bodies compressed and urgent. 'What was your biggest fear about having a daughter?' I asked, and the wind seemed to blow then, a soft push.

Without a breath between thought, Mum replied, 'It was

keeping you safe. I wanted to protect you from any harshness, and the older you got the harder it was. Every time you walked out the door I was scared you wouldn't come back. Or that something out there would hurt you.' And she reached her tiny hand out. 'Do you worry about being a daughter?' Mum asked.

'Yep. All the time. I worry that all the dreams you had for me, I will waste. Or that how I see myself is not as powerful as you wanted. Truth is, I have spent my life moving away from you, in order to become myself. Yet all the minutes are really turning me into the best parts of who you are.'

'Dare,' Mum said.

'Come on,' I shouted, and we jumped up knowingly, running to the front of the house.

Mum started the ignition, I turned the radio on and we reversed out, until the garden was behind us, a jumble of wind and trees. We drove for a while, through the back-of-the-hand roads, past the chip shop, the park. And in some moments, when we felt scared or unsure, the sunlight flashed our reflections back and forth across the glass and we saw ourselves, and each other, as if for the very first time.

In a Fever of Days

---

an ode to my mother

My mother, your kitchen
is a recovery room, where we bend
over rust coloured tea, and pour
boiling conversation out.

I have already opened up
your cupboards for kettle chips,
the fridge for the fancy brie,
now we sit, the tap still reliably
letting go. I hand you over another
heartache to mend

and you smile at my youth, flashing
a space where a tooth once grew.
In a fever of days, after all these years,
you still shock me with your wisdom.

If I am ever to have a child
and she was even half your kindness,
I know my body would have made
a good solid thing.

I will tell her, Mother,
how your words always
met my emergency, then became
the cure for my wounds.

A Big Beautiful Joke

The Genealogist calls me back:
'I've discovered a man fitting your
great-grandfather's name, who lived
in Bristol before moving to London
and having a family there.'

I am seven years old.
The same age
my mother was when she breathed
that orphanage into form.
We have left Margate behind, the hope
of slot machines and afternoons
trying every flavour
of childhood rebellion, so to settle
just outside Bristol.
We have no reason to be here.

The Genealogist tells me the names
of the roads my South African great-
grandfather worked on, the street
in which he lived. I shake the magic
from the phone and dance on it.

I am seventeen years old. I have swapped
the outskirts of Bristol for the middle of it all.
I make use of myself in cafés, sweat the floors
of broody drum and bass nights, take myself
to heart. I have no reason to be here.

I am thirty-three when I learn his streets
are the same streets I have spent my life
belonging to. The roads I have worked on,
the house he lived in,
a throw away from my own.

And when the Genealogist and I hang up
the phone, I press my palm against my mouth,
lips in the shape of a cylinder, a noise flung
into the beginning of sound. Hand pulled away,
a round of laughter, the collapse of head onto table,
the face a stage, the whole world
a big, beautiful joke –

one in which I have left Bristol for South Africa
in search of something already here.
One in which everything returns to the start
and none of us have grounds
to make home in this place.
But for some reason we still keep
the hall light on at night.
In case they want to come through
and see
all the miracles inside.

Singing the Songs of Our Mothers

_____

*I asked individuals from seven different countries,
'What is your mother's song'?*

Our mother's song alone: smoking out a window, wearing red
lipstick for the moon. Our mother's song for lost lovers, lost keys,
for those teenagers wearing the faces of lost time.

Your mother's song longing to fit that yellow dress, gasping into
her jeans, agreeing on salad, aching for substance. Your mother's
song a kitchen of red wine and Beyoncé's waist spinning.

Their mother's song a war cry, an activist's banner, a protest before
bed that moved them into revolution by the next morning. Their
mother's song chanting a bill of change, shooting them from sleep.

His mother's song unaware. A secret hum set to washing up.
A whistle as the mop trailed behind the clothesline, how soft
her sound blew through it, how quiet her voice made the beds.

Her mother's song as Tina Turner's sequins. High heels
cluttering the lino, squeezing out high notes for everyone
to hold. Something that shakes us deep beneath the marrow.

Or could it be in the gaps left behind? Something soundless
and stuck, removing furniture because nowhere's comfortable
anymore. A single parent surviving on lullabies alone.

His mother's song slept in a barn with no roof, ate pilchards
and problems. It became a verse for the working classes, it knew
the grating of teeth, knew the underdog, knew how to bark.

It was the song that struck a match: we, the children
who became people of the world. How she set us
all alight, a blaze of purpose, full of unstoppable power.

Cut Up and Shared Around

My aunty, the youngest one, says,
'Why would I want to talk to you about my parents or my grandparents?
They didn't want me.'

So I turn to my other aunty, the oldest one, and she says,
'That's not true. Our mum tried for twelve months before we were taken
away by the authorities.'

Strange how this huge detail had never been cut up and shared around.

I tell my mother,
'She never gave you away. You were taken. It wasn't that she didn't want you;
she wasn't allowed to have you,'

and my mother, she smiles,
but stares for a long time, out of the window,
into the vanishing day.

Children Who Unfolded in the Light

Mum says: I remember her beautiful,
but doesn't every child look at her mother
like she was the first woman formed?

She was cloud-soft, didn't lift her voice
at us once. Gentle-natured, she bore
our eyes. Her skin was the soil dug

and when he scattered the earth,
her stomach bloomed, then broke
with five children. Children who unfolded

in the light. She grew us all from air.
And when he left, her hair became
the crows who fought then flew, stormed

the garden with wing and beak, ate
everything alive. Her mouth was petals
plucked then held out in the heat, her ankles

roots pulled. Her heart, oh, her heart,
I'm sure it was the sun, it's what made
us glow. I was seven years old,

how time flies,
when I watched her fade away,
the last time I saw her rise.

The School of Loss

My sweet, imagined grandmother;
a woman in all places
and no place at all –

under apricot trees,
in apple orchards,
near the boozy figs.

Ladybirds swarm her cheeks, bees
stumble from her ears, nectar spills
from each of her steps.

How tight she holds my hand,
teaches me the mess of cooking,
how to flirt using my fingers

and I stick to her side, to her honey-
comb hips, like Blu Tack
sticks on the back of a paper heart.

*

In dreams, my grandfather
is a dead-end, a cul-de-sac of cement
and mortar I cannot pass through.

Or he's a field of corn, where we play
hide-and-seek, rushing the avenues
of barley, until we find one another.

In that hour of golden light, his voice,
erratic as jazz, smells like a twist of lime
and salt. Sometimes we dance together,

my head in bits on his shoulder,
his arms holding me loose enough
so that I can still breathe,

but tight enough
so he can never again
let me go.

Wind Phone

I drag a wind-up phone
into my garden. It's plastic,
bright red and beautiful,
the numbers dizzying

themselves as I poke
my finger in and dial
the digits of dreams, hear
my own breath ringing back.

I feel stupid, speaking out
this odd ritual of sound,
silence returned when all
I want is a loud round of karaoke,

the entire Earth joining in.
Yet I wear my best voice,
keep rolling language between
teeth and tongue. Lose myself

in questions. Ask how they are,
do they have a flat in heaven,
with photographs of us grinding
our grins? Ask if they eat

the meals we offer
up to them in prayer.
Ask how they could
have forgotten my mother.

Nothing is forgotten, the wind says back.
You always remember what was made inside of your being.
It howls, How perfect her body once felt in my arms.
How tight I would hold her to my chest.

The Sofa

Make-believe a sofa, big enough for the three of us,
my grandmother, mother and me. In this version

there is no orphanage, only us women,
a strong sense of family threading us at the sides.

The dresses my mother once made me as a child,
we each wear a different size, polka dot with a stitch

of colour; we can barely talk through giggling.
But Grandmother always knits

the conversation back to my beautiful brother
and the love she feels for the great-grandchildren

he has made her. The room smells of burnt coffee,
of okra fried and hot bread; there are books

piled on shelves and plants spilling on tables, lamps
and huge open windows with curtains that roll

in the talkative wind. In this version, we are mended,
rich in company, our futures podgy and elastic.

From the radio Ella Fitzgerald swoons
and my grandmother shifts excitedly

in her seat, gathers our hands, sways to the sound.
She teaches us a sentence, and we sing it back,

imagine that: my grandmother's voice filling
the entirety of our lives.

How My Mother's Song Might Sound

It is not a blues band, complex and melodic, becoming in a New
Orleans bar. It is not a bar at all, although it is packed,
mood lighting and Campari muddled.

It's a solo, maybe with piano, maybe with nothing at all.
A choir, busy and brave. It is London, Bristol, South Africa,
a constellation of enter and return,

of places that seem to grow with each retelling.
It is not golden, not hot spotlight and fame, it has been red
at times, it's the rhythm of people

falling in and out of love. Though it's not stuck in one place,
it's an ever-moving sound, it is looking back
to dance in a new direction.

It's not an old eighties shell suit, thin and luminous. It is a dress,
fallen to the floor, an entire body bare and free. It's a new face
that allows the old stories to migrate through the temples.

A face that turns itself towards the window,
regardless of what it might see this time,
and lets the light flood through.

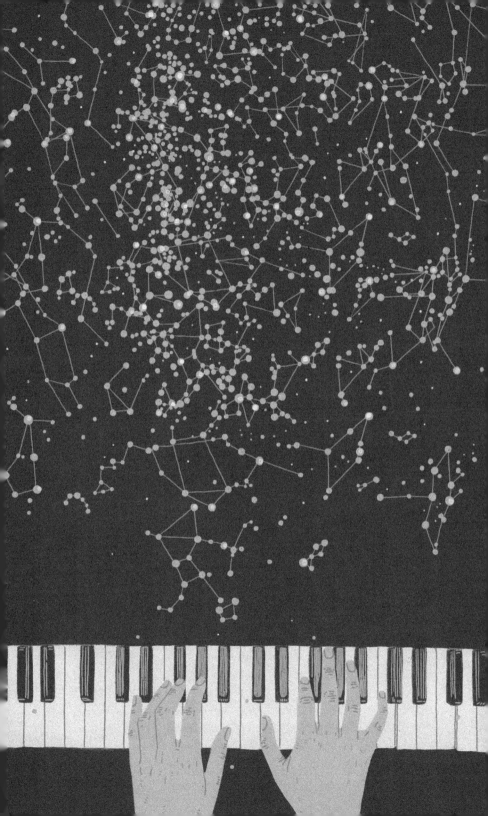

Baby Steps

It's raining, so I call a taxi and the driver collects me from home. We haven't been driving long when he asks what I'm doing today. I tell him about the book, how important this afternoon is. I have found my mother's cousins. Both in the UK, both as ecstatic as a party popper to hear from me. When I told my mother I'd discovered them, she said she'd forgotten they existed. 'Until an inquisitive daughter came along with a hunger for gaps and Sellotape and started asking questions.' Mum has not seen them since age seven when she went into the orphanage. She is seventy-five this year; that is sixty-eight years of waiting. She is all kinds of happy. When I tell him this, the taxi driver is all kinds of happy too. He says:

'My father died five years ago, totally out of the blue. A month later I received a phone call from Ethiopia. I remember it was mostly sounds from the back of the throat. Those inaudible to the normal human ear, yet in times of challenge you fine-tune to every nuance, don't you? You are able to hear all the aching. It was a stranger on the other end. An unfamiliar voice. The voice tells me, *I am your half-brother.*'

Red light, we stop for moments, the repetition of sirens and he keeps turning to face me, like he is collecting my expressions. The city is a disco ball, lightning shows off in outbursts, and here we are between shadow and sun.

'So, the story goes that my father had a child, a boy, before he met my mother. But my mother never knew about him. None of us did.' He indicates without looking at the road, it is second nature to him, swinging through the Bristol streets, eyes shift between everything and nothing.

'My sister has fully embraced him, she calls him brother, even though we have never met in the flesh. When she says his name it sounds like she has always said it. For me it sounds like choking, coughing out something strange and painful that is stuck. I am not sure how to celebrate what I didn't know existed. Something that makes me feel so much sadness.'

Then the city is a sponge leaking water. He pulls over and briefly we sit. He wishes me luck. I wish him a good onward journey. I am minutes before meeting them and there are so many songs on the radio that I do not know which one is trying to tell me something. Finally the tuner settles on Radio 1 and fucking Steps are singing us away. They're right; it is a tragedy sometimes – all this unwrapping, all this discovery.

The taxi driver and I have found our commonality, where small talk leaves and something big enters. He has spoken of everything I have been feeling, of how strange it is to re-welcome into your life that which you never knew existed. And I am going to meet the family he hasn't been able to bring himself to face yet. We let the music continue. Beyond the tragedy there is hope, there is glitter, fake tan and a monotonous soundtrack. I climb out and he nods, indicates himself away, seemingly so sure of where he is headed next.

My mother's cousins and I meet in a bar on the Harbourside and for the next six hours I hang out with three little girls in grown-up costumes, all giddy and giggling.

'Real family,' my mother says, holding them against her like another skin. And I think of the taxi driver and wonder if I should invite him along to this. I begin with a note, scribble it out on a beer mat. Once finished I consider more people I want to be here and I start to write invites for them all. I suggest they bring partners, friends, kids. I sit and wait, watching these women become young again in front of me.

The invited, they start turning up; first it's a few hundred, then they arrive in huge floods, crowds pushing through the double doors, queues wiggling around the city. We cram into the bar. I roll out the mini quiches and pineapple on sticks, welcome in the DJ who fills the records with his own voice. It's getting real busy now, uncles and aunts, children running around in circles, so many familiar faces alongside so many strangers. Steps have just arrived. H is wearing gold hotpants, Claire looks flawless. They begin to perform in those tight routines and synchronised voices. We are dancing now, everyone is here, all seven and a half billion of us, spilling out onto the streets, twirling and spinning each other, laughing and moving at this one family party.

And some of us hurt, and some of us are sad, and some of us are in shock, and some of us do not know if we should laugh or cry, and some of us feel wanted, and some of us don't, and some us hold strange names in our mouths, yet here we are together, through it all, in utter celebration.

Notes

The Ventriloquist's Voice is also published in *Magma 74*, July 2019.

A Flood of Men and a Few Different Languages:
'Apartheid was characterised by an authoritarian political culture based on baasskap (or white supremacy), which encouraged state repression of Black African, Coloured, and Asian South Africans for the benefit of the nation's minority white population.'
–Mayne, Alan. From *Politics Past to Politics Future: An Integrated Analysis of Current and Emergent Paradigms*. Westport, Connecticut: Praeger, 1999.

More information on the project, including films and audio, can be found at www.singingmymotherssong.com

Acknowledgments

Thank you to all who continually support my work, be it reading it, watching it, informing it or finding themselves inside it.

Thank you to the Arts Council UK for funding Singing My Mother's Song. You have allowed me to bring to fruition a dream I didn't even know needed to be awakened. To Saskia Watkin for the support with the funding application. You are a total boss.

To Hannah Lowe and Tania Hershman for your epic editing skills. As writers and women, I admire you both immensely. To Larissa Koutakos for journeying with me to South Africa at the very last minute and being the best travelling partner ever. Thank you to Caroline, the Genealogist, for your research and role in this work.

To all the phenomenal artists who have collaborated on this project: Toni Stuart, Malika Ndlovu, Jim Demuth, Nyaniso Dzedze, Yana Fay Dzedze, Dominie Hooper. To the endless Anna Higgie. I so love working with you and your immense talent.

Thank you to all my dear friends and teachers. Naela, Michelle, Thando, Saima, Anna, Jenny, Jonathan, Ursula, Alice, Muriel, Hannah, Amanda, Josiane, Nanna. Thank you, Jamie Catto, Carie Matthias, Ahmad Dede Pattisahusiwa, the Devo and Deep Inner Knowing Posse for your guidance. Thank you, Kesty, for all those years of learning this story inside me. Thank you to Raul for your continued support and belief in me and my work. Thank you, Jay, for being my philosophical sounding board. Thank you, Lucy English, for all the opportunities. Thank you, Marcus, for the inspiration. Chicken for teaching me unconditional love. I could go on and fill the pages of this book with those I admire, respect and value in my life. And there are so many. I hope you all deeply know who you are.

To those who answered the question 'What is your mother's song?' and were brave enough to let me access and use your story in the retelling of my own, I am so grateful.

Thanks to the poetry community as a whole and all the amazing artists that fill it. You are a warm bowl of something comforting. Special props to Sally Reader and Vanessa Kisuule; you're my poetry babes. I am so grateful for your love, support and friendship.

Thank you to Burning Eye, from the bottom of me, for providing so much for so many poets. Thank you to the Arvon Foundation; the time writing with you was invaluable in the forming of this collection.

To Bath Spa University, UK; to Wits University, Johannesburg, and all the team who work there. Thanks to all my students everywhere. I learn myself daily through you. To Reuann and all at the Nelson Mandela Bay, Lyn from uMzantsi and the amazing Lelethu. You are poetry.

Last but not least, thank you to my family. All the aunties and uncles in this collection. To the family now discovered and the ones who have been lost along the way. To my ancestors; it is with your quiet and loud guidance this collection was possible and our family narrative has forever shifted. And finally, thanks to my mother, Maggie, the first and last person I collapse into. For letting me tell this story. For being the most badass woman I know. Strong. Soft. Forever an inspiration to so many. I love you.

To everyone holding this book, I hope if nothing else it may serve to remind that in our ordinary lives, we have the chance to redefine the past and then change our possible futures.

REBECCA TANTONY

Rebecca Tantony is a writer and facilitator driven to understand the messy and wild human experience in greater depth. Living and working in Bristol, she has been commissioned by the BBC and Radio 4, and her writing has been described as 'mesmerising' in the Guardian. She is the author of collections Talk You Round Till Dusk (Burning Eye, 2015) and All The Journeys I Never Took (Burning Eye, 2017). In 2016 she received an MA in creative writing and a distinction for her final manuscript. In 2017 she toured an Arts Council funded one-on-one immersive spoken word show, under the same title as her second collection

Rebecca has work in various anthologies, journals and magazines such as Mslexia, Oh Comely and Bare Fiction, and has read in numerous venues including the Royal Albert Hall, the Natural History Museum and Southbank Centre. She has performed at music and literary festivals throughout the UK, and poetry readings have taken her to Turkey, India, America, Sweden and Germany.

Rebecca is currently teaching the Performance Poetry module and creative writing to BA students at Bath Spa University. She has been writer in residence for various institutes and organisations, including First Story and Wits University, Johannesburg. She has taught workshops in schools as part of the secondary curriculum, and outside schools to those excluded from education, ex-offenders, refugee groups and the elderly. She wholeheartedly believes that everyone has a story that deserves to be heard.

www.rebecca-tantony.com

ANNA HIGGIE

Anna Higgie is an Australian-born illustrator now living and working in Bristol. Anna spends most of her time in her Stokes Croft studio where she uses a combination of traditional and digital techniques to create her illustrations.

After studying painting and fine art at the National Art School in Sydney, Anna went on to study illustration and typography in London.

She has worked with many clients in the UK and abroad including British Vogue, Vanity Fair Paris, Laurence King Publishing, the Guardian, the Financial Times, Penguin Books, Random House, Planet Mu Records, GQ Japan, Green Man Festival and the National Institute of Fashion, Italy. She has been a featured artist in Taschen's Illustration Now! and Illustration Now! Fashion series.

@annahiggie

Lightning Source UK Ltd.
Milton Keynes UK
UKHW022331010819
347223UK00006B/70/P